Wonderful Designs
for Scrapbooks

Wonderful Designs for Scrapbooks

Ideas & Inspiration to Enhance Your Treasured Photos

MEGAN FLOWERS SKEELS

Sterling Publishing Co., Inc. New York
A Sterling/Chapelle Book

Chapelle, Ltd., Inc., P.O. Box 9252, Ogden, UT 84409
    P. O. Box 9252, Ogden, UT 84409
    (801) 621-2777 • (801) 621-2788 Fax
    e-mail: chapelle@chapelleltd.com
    Web site: www.chapelleltd.com

           Library of Congress Cataloging-in-Publication Data

Skeels, Megan Flowers.
    Scrapbooking from a designer's perspective / Megan Flowers
Skeels.
        p. cm.
    "A Sterling/Chapelle Book."
    Includes index.
    ISBN-13: 978-1-4027-2877-8
    ISBN-10: 1-4027-2877-8
    1. Photograph albums. 2. Photographs--Conservation and
restoration. 3. Scrapbooks. I. Title.
    TR465.S6 2006
    745.593--dc22
                                              2005032252

10 9 8 7 6 5 4 3 2 1
Published by Sterling Publishing Co., Inc.
387 Park Avenue South, New York, NY 10016
©2006 by Megan Flowers Skeels
Distributed in Canada by Sterling Publishing
c/o Canadian Manda Group, 165 Dufferin Street
Toronto, Ontario, Canada M6K 3H6
Distributed in the United Kingdom by GMC Distribution Services,
Castle Place, 166 High Street, Lewes, East Sussex, England BN7 1XU
Distributed in Australia by Capricorn Link (Australia) Pty. Ltd.
P.O. Box 704, Windsor, NSW 2756, Australia
Printed and Bound in China
All Rights Reserved

Sterling ISBN-13: 978-1-4027-2877-8
        ISBN-10: 1-4027-2877-8

For information about custom editions, special sales, premium
and corporate purchases, please contact Sterling Special Sales
Department at 800-805-5489 or specialsales@sterlingpub.com

Every effort has been made to ensure that all information in this book is accurate. However, due to differing con-
ditions, tools, and individual skills, the publisher cannot
be responsible for any injuries, losses, and/or other dam-
ages, which may result from the use of the information in
this book.

This volume is meant to stimulate decorating ideas. If
readers are not proficient in a skill necessary to attempt a
project, we urge that they refer to an instructional book
specifically addressing the required technique.

For my mom,
Pamela Flowers

Contents

Introduction

I have been drawn to scrapbooking ever since I was a child. Like many who love this art form, I wanted to chronicle a personal story. To create my first albums, I relied heavily on magazine cutouts and stickers. You have to look closely to tell that the pages are mine. Like the work of most beginners, the albums show little more than the seeds of what would grow into my personal style.

Over time, I came into my own. I watched how my mom, interior designer Pam Flowers, worked. Her sophisticated approach to creating distinctive settings for everyday life made me realize that scrapbook pages are like rooms and that the same principles she applied to interiors can help make every scrapbook a masterpiece. I started experimenting with different styles and materials, and the pages I created reflected my growing confidence as I learned how to balance risk and restraint. As an undergraduate at the University of Arkansas, I studied Art and started combining the techniques I learned with an interior design approach to scrapbooking.

More than ten years ago, I made an album for my sister Cara. When others saw it and requested that I make albums for them, my business Chronicles was born. Now it's my full-time job to find ways to help other people tell their stories. My clients give me boxes of photographs and I create unique handcrafted heirlooms that I hope they will be proud to pass down through the generations.

I scrapbook because I believe our stories are like us—unique, significant, and beautiful just the way we are. In a world where everything seems to be mass-produced, one of the best ways to honor those we love is by telling their stories with a designer's care for composition, color, texture, and style. This book will show you how to use key principles of interior design to create pages that transcend fads and can carry the story of your family's life far into the future.

Our stories are like us—unique, significant, and beautiful. Telling them with a designer's care will help future generations appreciate their value.

11

Composing the Page

When I first began scrapbooking, I had a tendency to build my pages haphazardly, layering stickers and tags as I went. The result of this lazy, thoughtless approach was predictable. Instead of pages that helped others (including my future self) experience the essence of a valued memory, I ended up with pages on which elements competed for attention. They pulled the eye every which way and sometimes even conveyed a mood that clashed with the events and expressions in the photographs.

As a scrapbook designer, however, I now approach each page deliberately. I don't rush it; I take the time to study the photograph or photographs and think about what the message should be and how to express it through the language of images. The difference between creating without a design versus creating with one is like that between a home into which you cram any old furniture and a home decorated with an eye for how it all goes together. Taking care to identify the desired effect and select and arrange elements so that they create that effect is composition, the art of careful planning. Just as composition is the heart of good interior design, so too can it give new life to your scrapbooking.

THINKING LIKE AN INTERIOR DESIGNER

"Planning" can mean different things to different people. For some, having a general intention in the back of one's mind counts as a plan. Not so for the interior designer. Materials are too expensive and time too precious to waste on a trial-and-error approach. Furthermore, an interior designer typically has a client to please. To prevent costly errors in judgment, the interior designer presents ideas in a tangible form such as through sketches and samples posted on a display board.

If the designer has done her or his job well, the client can imagine clearly the intended outcome and give well-informed approval of the work—or request changes—before the designer has invested too many resources in the project. While scrapbookers don't need to go to quite these lengths, developing a plan is the keystone to a designer approach. Sketching the design and laying out elements before committing to their placement can help you achieve the look you want.

When my mom, Pam Flowers, designed a roundabout sofa for an entrance hall, her brainstorming process happened as she sorted through fabrics and trims. To ensure that her selections would work, she physically placed samples together and gave herself time to evaluate the results. Your scrapbook pages can benefit from similar treatment.

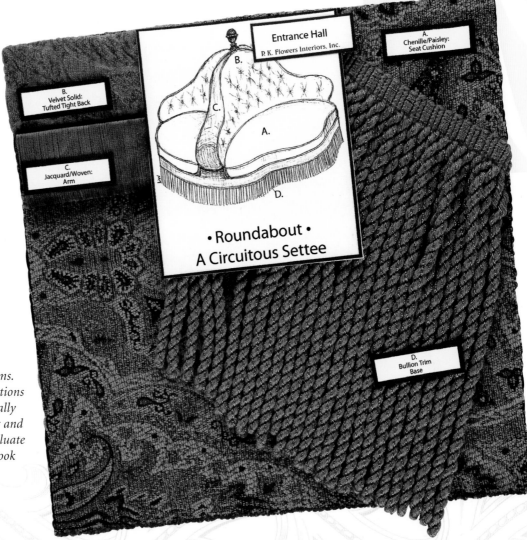

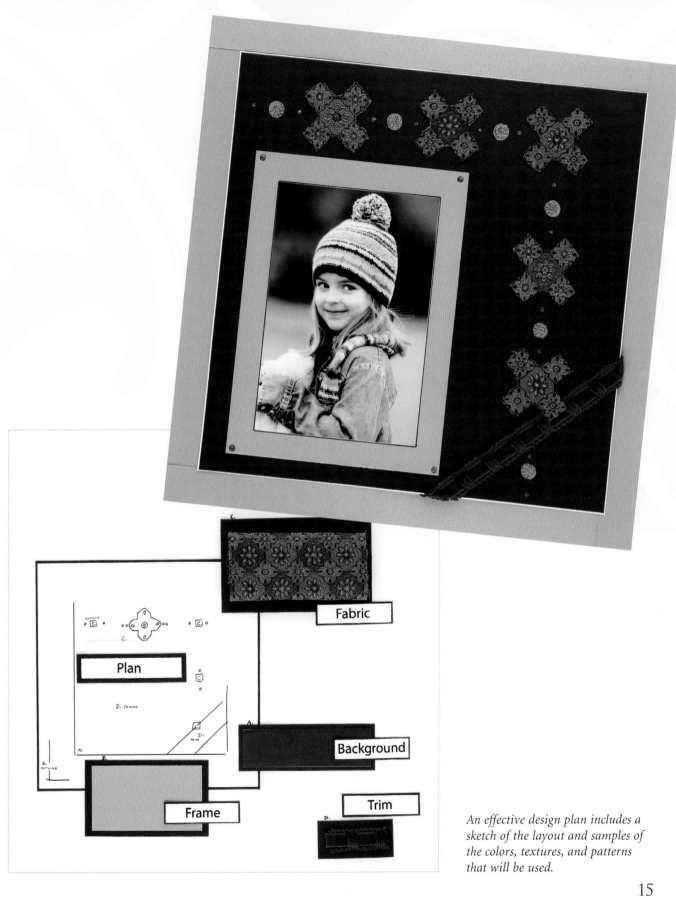

An effective design plan includes a sketch of the layout and samples of the colors, textures, and patterns that will be used.

IDENTIFY THE KEY ELEMENT

To create beautiful, tasteful pages that reflect your intentions, I suggest approaching your pages the way an interior designer creates a scheme for a room. Interior designers typically begin with a key piece such as a painting or a sofa, and then select elements that coordinate with it. The key piece for a scrapbook page is the photograph. Assess its visual qualities such as the dominant colors and the depth of contrast between dark and light. Consider also the subject and the essence of the person or event it celebrates. Ultimately, the photograph will dictate the design of your page.

Although there are three photographs on this layout, the key element is really the image in the center. Notice how it is emphasized by a raised position and the vertical lines of the flower petals below.

MAKE YOUR SPACE COUNT

Whether a room is large or small, a smart designer looks to make every inch of it work. That means no dead space, no blah corners. Objects are positioned to bring your eye to the focal point either quickly or slowly, depending on the overall effect desired. From the ceiling to the floor, from wall to wall, an interior designer makes each section of space count.

Since the typical scrapbook page is only a single square foot, it's even more important for a scrapbooker to know how to use space well. Do this by making sure every element contributes to the overall design. Select items carefully and place them strategically. Look at how a page can be divided into halves and quarters. What happens when you place a large element on the centerline and a small one on a margin? What happens when you switch the elements? As you work out your design, consider the various ways you can use the space.

Making space count doesn't mean filling up every corner—it means making relatively empty spaces a clear part of the design.

It took approximately two hours to design this composition, but I feel that the finished product was worth the careful planning. Notice how the borders of flowers and dots make the eye move around the page without pulling it away from the focal point—the absolute joy in my niece Adelaide's expression.

Again, the composition is built around the photograph. To echo the boy's position within the photo, I placed the photo on the left side of the page and selected green, brown, and gold to make his pink cheeks and bright eyes all the more striking.

STRIKING A BALANCE

When asked, many interior designers will say a well-balanced design just "looks right." While we often use intuition to achieve a balanced look, we can hone this intuition with an awareness of different kinds of balance. Symmetry uses mirror images on either side of a centerline to create balance and give the design a formal, cultivated quality. Asymmetrical balance places the focal point off-center and tends to be more dynamic as it invites the viewer's eye to travel between different points on the page. Many designs combine both types of balance to play the stabilizing effect of symmetry against the surprises of asymmetry.

The branches and twin sides of this dresser provide a symmetry that offsets the asymmetrical touches, such as the hats.

The symmetrical bows lend a formal, classic appeal to this layout while the asymmetrical placement of the photo adds a fresh, contemporary touch.

To understand how balance works in design, think of a seesaw. To achieve a symmetrical balance, you need two people of the same weight to sit an equal distance from the center. In scrapbooking terms, symmetrical balance is achieved when all elements on both sides of the centerline match in look and placement.

If the people on the seesaw are not the same weight, they can achieve an asymmetrical balance by adding a third person to the lighter side or by moving the heavier person closer to the center. When it comes to design, elements can be perceived as heavy or light depending on their size, color, texture, and placement relative to one another. For example, something small and dark on one side of a page may balance something larger and light-colored.

When a seesaw is unbalanced, one end of it goes down and stays put. An unbalanced design stagnates because the elements don't carry the eye around the page in a strategic way. Use symmetry and asymmetry with awareness to create well-balanced pages.

Radial symmetry is balance achieved around a central point. I call this type of layout "scrapbooking in-the-round." Radial symmetry can be mesmerizing with its ability to pull the eye to the center.

PLAYING WITH LINE

Whether decorating a home or creating a page, the designer uses lines to direct the viewer's attention and create the desired effect. For instance, the straight vertical line of a column symbolizes stability and permanence, and grants your design a formal quality. Horizontal lines, however, encourage the eye to travel across the page. They tend to bring a sense of movement to the design. Curved lines yield softness and motion, like a meandering stream.

Explore how vertical, horizontal, and curved lines can be used to draw the eye around the focal point, which on this page is in the center.

(Above) The painted horizontal lines on the background complement the landscape orientation of the photograph and the relaxed image of the girls.

(Right) This nook combines soothing curves and horizontal lines with the energy of vertical plants and statues.

24

NOTICING SCALE

When an interior designer approaches a room, scale is always at the forefront of her or his mind. Scale is the relationship of the size each element has to the others within an overall scheme. While you can play with proportion to emphasize and deemphasize different parts of your composition, it generally looks more appealing when you select elements to scale. For instance, an eight-foot-long sofa makes a small room seem uncomfortably crowded. Likewise, a large room with tiny furniture may seem empty or strange, like something out of *Alice in Wonderland*.

When designing a scrapbook page, scale is no less important. Consider the size of your page and select elements accordingly. A large floral background or numerous embellishments may not show to advantage on a six-inch-square page and a narrow bit of ribbon may be dwarfed on a larger layout. Aim to strike a balance between the size and number of photographs and the decorations around them.

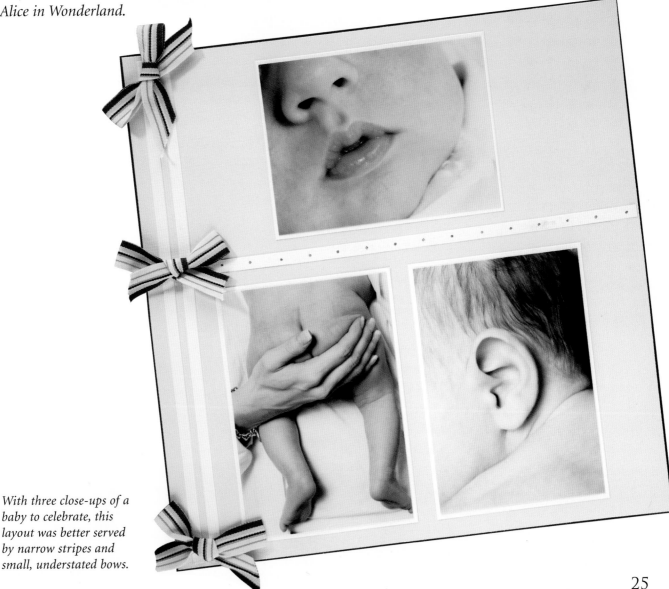

With three close-ups of a baby to celebrate, this layout was better served by narrow stripes and small, understated bows.

PROJECT

Dynamic Background Page

Materials

- 12" square of watercolor paper
- Blue, bronze, green, and white acrylic paints
- Paintbrush
- Water

Instructions

STEP ONE

Use a dry brush to spread dabs of blue paint on the paper.

STEP TWO

Repeat Step One to apply a layer of green paint.

STEP THREE

Repeat Step One to apply a layer of bronze paint.

STEP FOUR

Apply a wash of diluted white paint over the entire page. When dry, add blue accents.

STEP ONE

STEP TWO

STEP THREE

STEP FOUR

Bring energy to a symmetrical layout with a free-form painted background page.

summer

Color Confidence

It's impossible to overestimate the importance of color. Color brings glory to springtime blooms and serenity to a seascape. It enriches a holiday table and adds cheer to midwinter. Interior designers wield the power of color to evoke a desired mood. Rich and formal? Perhaps mellow golds and deep wines. Fresh and crisp? White, apple green, and robin's egg blue are recent favorites. Cozy and cheerful? Bright orange might be the ticket.

Although people have different personal and cultural associations with colors, we often share similar responses on a basic level. For example, fiery hues such as orange and red tend to excite. Yellow cheers us, like the sun. Green and blue—the colors of fresh plants and cool water—are restful and serene, while dark violet can seem as mysterious as a shadowy cave.

As you design each scrapbook page, consider the emotional impact you want it to have and choose colors to help you achieve it. Convey an exuberant spirit with a simple, bright color scheme; for moody, complex subjects, a sophisticated blend of dusky colors may be better. Also consider the relationship of color to the technical side of your design: you can highlight or downplay elements with a strategic use of color.

UNDERSTANDING COLOR

If you've ever had an art class, chances are you were introduced to a color wheel. This tool helps artists and designers identify the relationships between the primary colors red, yellow, and blue, and the hues in between. When you combine two or more primary colors, you get secondary colors such as orange, green, and violet. Colors made from blending a primary with a secondary color are called tertiary colors—and it goes on from there.

SELECTING COLOR
SCHEMES

Color schemes can be simple or elaborate. It's all a matter of what experience you want to create. For instance, a single color displayed in a range of intensity foregrounds the essence of that color. The simplicity of monochromatic color can result in a classic understated look that subtly highlights texture and pattern.

If you want a more complex color scheme, but fear you may be tempted to go overboard, experiment with analogous colors. To identify analogous colors, aim for those that are near each other on the color wheel. For example, the range of color between one primary color such as blue and a nearby secondary color such as green is "analogous." Limiting your palette to analogous colors can help you unify your page.

The many hues used in this page harmonize well because the palette relies chiefly on analogous greens and yellows. Touches of pink and purple— from the complementary red color family—bring out the color of the bride's skin.

For the most dramatic use of color, choose complementary hues. These are colors from opposite sides of the color wheel. By combining complementary colors, you intensify the brightness of each one and add dynamic energy to your design. Consider the bold impact of red berries against green branches or orange flowers held up to a blue sky. In fact, complementary colors offer such a high level of contrast that interior designers tend to use them only to amplify details and rely on pairings that aren't quite complementary for larger elements such as walls and furniture.

Consider adding touches of an intermediate hue such as gold to soften the strong contrast of complementary hues such as red and green.

If you find it difficult to coordinate colors, peruse the sample cards at a local paint store. Notice how a single hue such as orange can look pastel, smoky, or clear, depending on whether you add white, black, or leave the color pure. If your color combinations don't look quite right, you may be haphazardly pairing smoky shades with pastels or clears. Of course, it's fine to combine shades if you like the results, but it's usually better to build a palette in which most or all of the colors are of similar shades.

ACHIEVING UNITY AND EMPHASIS

One of color's greatest characteristics is that it enables a designer to unify elements so that the viewer sees the whole work, not just the individual parts. For instance, a single color such as red can be the common thread that weaves together many different aspects of a layout. You can also use contrasting colors to emphasize or counterbalance elements on a page and to highlight details that might otherwise fade into the background.

Texture

Texture is one of the fastest routes to someone's memories. No parent forgets the downy feel of a baby's head. Gritty sand brings back vacations at the beach, crisp brown leaves will always say "Fall," and matted faux fur recalls childhood winter boots. Defined simply, texture is the way a surface feels. It can be rough or smooth, hard or soft, matte or glossy. From the walls to the fabrics, and even to the floors, texture is a special part of interior design. The right use of texture invites us to move into a room and run our hands across the objects we find there.

As a scrapbooker, you can use texture to bring depth and richness to a flat page by combining different patterns and surfaces. Choose textures that match the subject of a page. For instance, when I create a page for a baby's christening, I choose fine lace and soft textiles. If the subject is a man, I may use suede, wool, and metal. To create a feeling of timelessness, I try to include textures that mimic the textures found on antique objects, such as patina. I know I've succeeded in my aim when a page inspires someone to move from looking to touching, as if the texture has pulled them in.

LAYERING

Interior designers layer materials to enhance the appearance of texture. While many scrapbookers are familiar with the technique of combining specialty papers, they often overlook the artistic freedom that comes with using paints, inks, and washes. To achieve customized effects, I may start with a painted or fabric background and load it with painted papers, each with a different type of surface.

Smooth pearls and a knobby brocade ribbon are simple yet effective ways to create rich texture.

Here, the stamp subtly adds richness to the page with variations of paint and pigments.

Stamping is another way to layer images and colors, producing a richer texture. Available at most craft stores, rubber and foam stamps come in a variety of motifs from botanicals, airplanes, and architectural designs to pretty much anything else. I use foam stamps, which are much less expensive than rubber stamps. I've found them to be durable as well—after more than forty impressions with my favorite four-point scroll motif, the stamp shows zero signs of wear. One of the best features of stamping is that you can achieve many different effects with a single stamp. You can apply fresh color after each impression to create the same look time and again, or allow the pigment to fade over multiple impressions. You can embellish an impression with jewels or outline the image with pen to produce the look of hand-drawn art.

PROJECT

Easy Layered Background

Materials

- 11" square of watercolor paper
- Blue ink
- Blue watercolor paint
- Bronze, sage, and white acrylic paints
- Ink wedge
- Paintbrush

Instructions

STEP ONE

Cover paper with bronze paint. Let it dry completely.

STEP TWO

Apply a wash of white paint over the entire page.

STEP THREE

Apply a wash of sage paint. Smear blue ink onto the surface, using an ink wedge and a loose stroke.

STEP FOUR

Use a dry brush to apply undiluted blue paint. Mount paint square on blue scrapbook paper.

STEP ONE

STEP TWO

STEP THREE

STEP FOUR

Bringing texture to your pages can be as simple as layering colors onto heavy watercolor paper to create a rich background.

FINDING INSPIRATION

When searching for new ways to add texture to your pages, you need look no further than to the walls, floors, and furniture in your home. Stucco, wallpaper, faux finishes, rugs, linoleum—consider the different effect produced by different materials. From sheer gauze to thick tapestry, smooth plastics and metals to rough suede, fabrics and notions give you a wealth of textures from which to draw great ideas. Many home textiles such as upholstery fabric lend themselves to direct application to a page. When this isn't practical, you can paint, draw, emboss, collage, and use other techniques to imitate the textures in your environment.

Turn to the textiles in your home for inventive ways to bring texture to your designs.

INCORPORATING THE DIMENSION OF TEXTURE

When interior designers speak of dimension, they're often referring to features that make you aware of a space as a three-dimensional experience. Ceiling fans hanging from a vaulted ceiling, swags framing an entryway, a richly colored painting peeking from a nook, inventive wall treatments—interior designers use countless ways to highlight the dimensionality of a space.

(Above) White columns and dark background walls emphasize the depth of this dining room's dimensions.

The height of the tassels and rich texture of the ribbon bring dimension to this page.

For the scrapbooker, dimension is in the grooves of a grosgrain ribbon and the height of a button's profile. Many of us already use items such as foam dots to bring dimension to our pages. But what else can we do to create richly textured projects? I suggest raiding the kitchen junk drawer and scouring tag sales for unique embellishments that bring three-dimensional interest to your work. Let friends know you collect small oddities, such as broken-off carvings and old jewelry.

To make dimension work for you, assess the weight and depth as well as the size of the object you intend to add to a page. Heavy objects can destroy a lightweight background paper, and embellishments with too high a profile may damage the pages around them (and make it impossible to close the album!).

You can also play tricks on the viewer's eye by creating false dimension. For instance, if you want to include a brass doorknocker on your page, try using a color copy instead of a real one. Or try painting shadows and highlights to lift two-dimensional drawings off the page.

PROJECT

Trompe l'oeil Design

Materials

- Cardstock
- Cream, lavender, pink, and white acrylic paints
- Fine-tipped black pen
- Paintbrush
- Pencil
- Scissors

Instructions

STEP ONE

Sketch an outline of your design onto cardstock. Cut it out.

STEP TWO

Place the shape onto your scrapbook page and trace. Fill in the outline with cream paint.

STEP THREE

When the base coat is dry, paint the crossing ties white and the spaces between the ties pale pink. Highlight the spaces between the ties with a little white for added dimension.

STEP FOUR

Paint a dark shade of pink to outline the interior shapes. Enhance the outlines with a fine-tipped black pen. Shade the spaces between the ties with a little lavender paint.

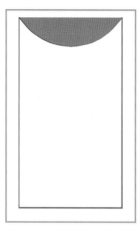

STEP ONE

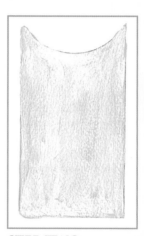

STEP TWO

STEP THREE

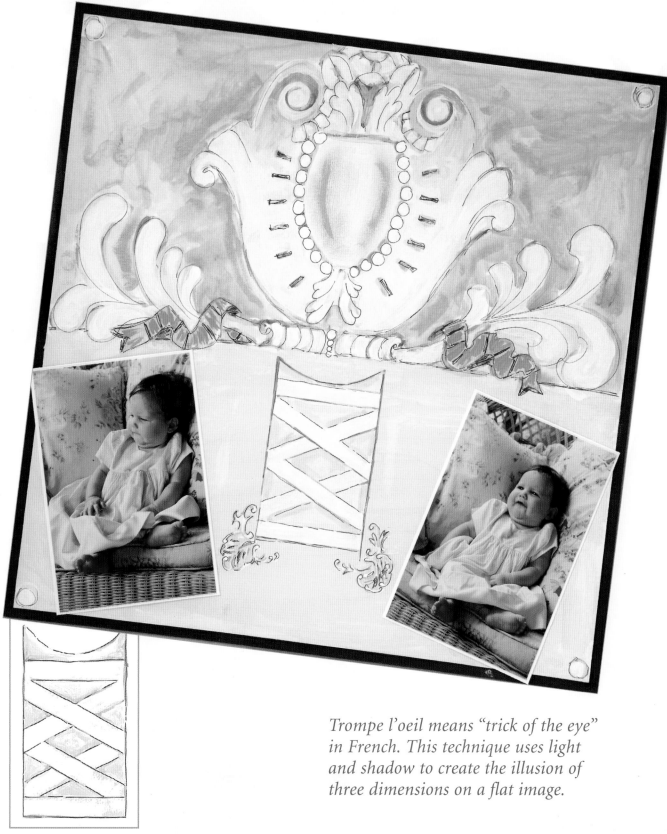

STEP FOUR

Trompe l'oeil means "trick of the eye" in French. This technique uses light and shadow to create the illusion of three dimensions on a flat image.

47

International Style

The world of design is truly a multicultural place. Not only do interior designers frequently turn to faraway places and other times for materials and inspiration, their clients often identify the look they want as "French Provincial," "Danish Modern," "Japanese Zen," and so on. Whether you're a seasoned traveler or just love the fantasy of escaping to a faraway place, consider how images and color schemes from around the globe can add excitement to your scrapbook pages, just as they add flair to the rooms of a home. By borrowing from international styles, you can journey from Morocco to Mexico with a flip of the page.

These days, I tend to use American, French, English, and Italian motifs. The depth of each country's design history could fill volumes. Though it is not the purpose of this book to delve deeply into these rich traditions, I do think it's worth mentioning some key elements of each.

AMERICAN COLONIAL

American traditions are often a patchwork of cultural influences, beginning with our British heritage. Since the Colonial period, we have gathered ideas from all over the globe. Still, a distinctively American style is often rooted in necessity and marked by beautiful simplicity and homespun touches such as stenciling and patchwork.

Nothing says American Country like an old crazy quilt. Here, the colors and textures of the quilt background are so rich and varied, there is no need for additional embellishment.

FRENCH FANTASY

To me, French style is playful, chic, and layered with history and sophistication. It is a style in which the obnoxious opulence of Louis XIV is at home alongside big sunflowers, fresh bread, and the easy vitality of a Paris café. As one designer puts it, the French have splendor and unshakeable style. In my own work, I play with my personal impressions of French style rather than try to capture "authentic" French style. It's my French fantasy, so to speak.

*Here, a French toile pattern in blue and off-white creates a French Country feel,
and ornate embellishments celebrate the French love of detail and elegance.*

BRITISH HISTORY

When I think of British design, I think of formal architectural details and those lovely English gardens. The formal qualities of a dark, velvet-lined parlor inspires my use of thick brocades and dark, wallpaper-like backgrounds.

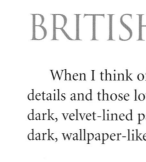

ITALIAN IDYLL

Italy is one of my favorite countries. Its history is filled with great artists, world-changing designs, and a warmth that only Italians can claim as their own. They are the masters of color, who invented the meaning of Old World charm. As an international leader in contemporary fashion as well as ancient art, Italy is a treasure chest for scrapbookers looking to infuse their pages with a fresh yet classic feel.

The stone arch in the photograph invited an Italian-inspired palette. To add warmth to the formal design, I painted an impression of a Tuscan villa.

PROJECT

Siena Marble Background

Materials

- 11" square of watercolor paper
- Acrylic glazing liquid
- Black pastel
- Brown, gold, sage, white, and yellow acrylic paints
- Paintbrush
- Tissue paper

Instructions

STEP ONE

Brush acrylic glazing liquid onto paper. Brush on gold paint. Use a dry paintbrush to smooth out the lines. Brush on yellow paint.

STEP TWO

Lift some of the wet paint, using a crumpled tissue. Apply "veins" of white paint, using the paintbrush. *Note: Keep your hand limp as you do this to achieve a loose, flowing effect.*

STEP THREE

When the surface is dry, outline the white veins with a black pastel. Draw pebbles or other organic forms along the black lines. Fill in the organic forms with white paint.

STEP FOUR

Surround the outlined forms with brown paint. Apply bronze and sage paint to add more depth to the design. Add gold and white paint as desired. To finish, retouch the black outlines.

STEP ONE

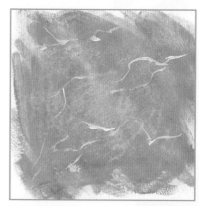

STEP TWO

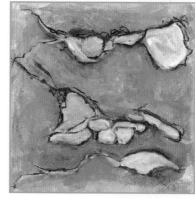

STEP THREE

STEP FOUR

The intense patterns and yellow color of the marble found in Siena, a town outside of Tuscany, create a classically Italian look.

FROM ROCOCO TO REGENCY ... AND BEYOND

Interior designers know that the way to innovation is through understanding and even borrowing from the past. They turn to other times as well as other places to discover refreshing combinations of design elements. Recently, I've gained styling ideas from such varied times as the era of Henry VIII, 1920s Paris, and the ruins of Pompeii. To expand your design horizons, try studying the flying buttresses of the Gothic Period, the Baroque flourishes of Versailles, or the neoclassical lines of Napoleonic France. The pages of history await you.

"Rococo" comes from the French word rocaille, or shell. Shell forms, curved lines, and delicate colors create the light and playful atmosphere that characterizes this style.

58

In the late eighteenth century, Europeans turned to ancient Greece for inspiration. This revival of an ancient style emphasized balanced proportions, clean lines, and harmonious colors. Here, clean lines and a delicate background color enhance this classical design.

The decoration of the Regency Period bordered on a frivolity that some designers have called "fussy exuberance." In this layout, Regency-inspired swags and tassels mirror the curved line of the woman's dress and reflect the playful element of a whispered conversation with a little girl.

During the Victorian Period, England celebrated a Gothic revival with dark colors and heavy interior trimmings and tapestries as well as details and patterns from other design periods.

PROJECT

Strié Panel Effect

Materials

- 12" square of watercolor paper
- 4¾" square of watercolor paper
- Circle stamp
- Foam dots
- Paintbrush
- Pencil
- Ruler
- Sponge
- Toothbrush
- Two shades of metallic antique silver paint

Instructions

STEP ONE

Draw a 6" square in the center of a 12" square of watercolor paper. Within the 6" square, draw a 5" square. Attach the 4¾" square of watercolor paper to the center of the 5" square, using foam dots.

STEP TWO

Mix each shade of paint with acrylic glazing liquid. Brush a different shade of mixed paint onto each square. Drag a toothbrush across the surfaces to create striations. When dry, use a dry sponge to scratch off some of the paint.

STEP THREE

Create a frame around the photo, using a circle stamp and white paint.

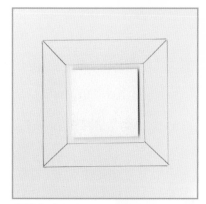

STEP ONE

STEP TWO

STEP THREE

Many European styles incorporate painted antiques with surfaces that show brushstrokes and color variation. Strié is a faux finishing technique that enables you to mimic this appealing look.

Artistic License

The great artists of the past were seekers whose desire for meaning, beauty, and change led them to find new ways of seeing the world and art. Given that their masterpieces help us to see the world in new ways too, it's no wonder that so many of us crave to have fine artwork in our homes. Interior designers are frequently asked to build a design scheme around a client's prized sculpture or painting. Though original works by well-established artists are out of reach for the average person, there's no reason we can't bring some of their genius into our lives by incorporating their images into our scrapbooks.

My personal favorites come from Impressionism and Post-Impressionism. Van Gogh, Cézanne, Monet, and Matisse used rich color and heavily textured brushstrokes to create works loaded with expressive power. For your own pages, find an artist whose work speaks to you and give yourself permission to have some fun while imitating their style. You may be surprised not only by the results but by how much you learn in the process.

One way to bring a work of art into your scrapbook is to select just a part of a famous painting that captures the essence of what you want in your design. For instance, I mimicked Vincent Van Gogh's brushstrokes and swirling constellations to pay tribute to Starry Night (1889).

Creating my version of Monet's Water Lilies (1909) brought me an even greater appreciation for the skill its apparent simplicity conceals. (My husband thought my water lilies were pickles!)

Henri Matisse relied on primitive forms, heavy outlines, and colors on flat planes to create passionate and expressive arrangements. I chose a portion of Harmony in Red (1908) to suffuse my page with its striking use of contrast between the warm red background and cool blue flowers.

This page borrows elements from Matisse's Decorative Figure on an Ornamental Ground *(1925). I ignored many of his details and concentrated primarily on his use of color and basic floral forms.*

PROJECT

Masterwork Page

Materials

- Art print image
- Paintbrush
- Paints
- Pencil
- Watercolor paper

Instructions

STEP ONE

Select an image such as *Sunflowers* by Van Gogh. Use the pencil to outline the main shapes of the chosen image on the watercolor paper. *Note: For beginners, I recommend choosing a model that has a relatively simple color scheme.*

STEP TWO

Add another level of detail to your artwork by drawing the outlines of smaller elements.

STEP THREE

Apply paint to the drawing. Aim to match colors and general placement, but don't worry about getting exact detail right.

STEP ONE

STEP TWO

STEP THREE

When you learn how to reproduce elements from your favorite paintings, you discover a new world of possibility.

Your Taste, Your Style

We've covered the basic principles of interior design that I have found most useful in my work as a scrapbook artist. Now there's only one thing missing: *you*. Whether planning a room or planning a page, the designer's approach brings together all the elements involved in a way no one else would.

Everyone has the ability to make their scrapbooks unique. Some of us lack the time or the inclination, and that's OK. But if fear is what holds us back, then we need to let loose. After all, if we don't like one page, we can always do another. (If you're worried about ruining precious photographs, that's what color copiers are for!)

My interior designer mom calls the discovery of one's unique style "coming home." Whether contemporary or vintage, bold or subtle, jam-packed or streamlined, your personal style is what will give your scrapbooks the mark of distinction that turns them into treasures. Give yourself permission to come home.

FINDING YOUR STYLE

Because my home reflects my love for antiques, I turn to it frequently for designs that enhance my work. Chances are, you already express your personal style through the way you decorate your living space. If this isn't the case—or if you'd like to change your style—try keeping a notebook or a file of magazine clippings, drawings, and fabric swatches that reflect your vision. As you become more aware of your taste, you can choose scrapbook designs to reflect it more accurately.

An easy way to bring your style to your pages is to borrow from the objects you love. Color photocopies on acid-free paper enable the scrapbooker to transform just about anything into easy-to-use images. I have photocopied book covers, vintage boxes, jewelry, aged wallpaper, fabrics, and other objects to create one-of-a-kind papers for my pages. Favorite trinkets also provide ideas for motifs. For instance, many antique boxes in my collection are graced with simple landscapes and beautiful floral arrangements that I have painted or drawn on my pages.

For rooms that reflect the occupants' interests, interior designers often decorate with objects used in a favorite pastime.

Yet another way to give scrapbooks a personal stamp is to apply the objects themselves to a page. Rather than throw away a scarf, a curtain, or a necktie that's been part of your life for years, why not incorporate it into your work?

GENERATIONAL DESIGN

Before antique hunting became the feverish trend that it is, my great grandmother made a study of old objects. My mom often accompanied Great-Grandma on her ventures, and later passed on a love for timeworn treasures to me. Mom's term for this transfer of taste is "generational design." Your family's generational design is reflected by the objects that have gained value simply by being loved and passed down, nicks and scratches notwithstanding. An example of generational design in action is when you give Aunt Louise's favorite vase a place of honor in your home, not just for the way it looks, but for the way its style is woven into your memories.

To me, generational design is an important aspect of scrapbooking in two ways. Looking at the objects you have come to love because they have been part of your family for generations can help you define your style. The scrapbook itself can also become a way to make your style available to future generations. With every scrapbook I make, I think about what qualities may inspire someone to pass it along and give its story and style a position of value in their family.

THE IMAGES AROUND YOU

When looking for ways to put your personal stamp on your designs, remember that good ideas can come from anywhere. I have been caught off guard by the source for a new layout so many times that I now routinely look in unlikely places. In addition to the pages of magazines on design, landscaping, and home trends, I've also found inspiration in shower curtains, retail shopping bags, advertisements, and jewelry catalogues. If you don't already keep a sketchpad handy or have a file of magazine clippings, you may want to get in the habit. Your next great idea may be right under your nose.

(Above) An architectural motif can be as close as the nearest wrought-iron fence.

(Left) You don't have to paint photographic-looking images to bring flowers, butterflies, and more to your pages.

By reducing garden flowers to their simplest shapes and colors, you can turn them into colorful backdrops for summertime photos.

To find your personal style, notice what colors, textures, and patterns you choose to surround yourself with, and seek ways to bring them to your scrapbook pages.

PROJECT

Two-tone Faux Patina

Materials

- 5" square of watercolor paper
- Acid-free spray fixative
- Acrylic glazing liquid
- Brown, gold, and white acrylic paints
- Paintbrush
- Sponge
- Tissue

Instructions

STEP ONE

Coat the 5" square of watercolor paper with white acrylic paint. When the base coat is dry, dab on acrylic glazing liquid, using a tissue and a dry sponge.

STEP TWO

Before the glazing liquid dries, brush white, gold, and a touch of brown paint, using quick loose strokes.

STEP THREE

Before the paint dries, use the technique described in Step Two to brush on more glaze and a darker layer of paint. Remove some of the paint with a tissue.

STEP FOUR

Drag a dry brush across the page to pull the paint in a horizontal direction. Spray the page with fixative to protect.

STEP ONE

STEP TWO

STEP THREE

82

STEP FOUR

Knowing how to create fabulous backgrounds enables you to express your personal style more easily. To get the most versatility from this technique, vary the colors and paper size and shape.

Tips for the Scrapbook Designer

Scrapbooking can be so much more than meets the eye. While the act of making a page can be fun and relaxing, my clients expect more from my work than the fact that I enjoy doing it. They expect—and I aim to create—a complete, tailor-made experience that makes a memory come alive for other people. When you too choose to make this your goal, you have accepted the designer's challenge.

Choosing to become a designer as well as a crafter of scrapbooks opens the door to an ongoing adventure. Not only will a designer's perspective change the appearance of your pages, it may very well change the way you see the world. Your mind as well as your eyes may open wider than ever. Suddenly colors appear brighter, shapes seem more striking, and materials you never noticed before are inspiring. In other words, your creativity blooms. Yet while being creative often means forgetting about the rigid rules in our heads, having a few principles to build from can help you achieve designs that stand the test of time. In this chapter, I offer a few suggestions based on what has worked for me.

Have a plan.

While designers are open to happy accidents and pleasant surprises, they also know that good designs take some forethought. Sketch your layout and place elements on the page before you glue them down to be sure your design is sound. It can save you time, materials, and frustration—and help you achieve unbelievable pages.

Design around a focal point.

Let the key feature—the photograph—help you choose the layout, colors, textures, and embellishments. Test each choice against whether it honestly enhances or detracts from the intended focal point of the design.

Frame key features.

Interior designers prevent key elements from fading into their surroundings by using frames. Whether you mount a photo on a square of paper or surround it with a mat, a frame emphasizes its importance and gives your album a more polished, professional appearance.

(Above) Even just a thin border of white and black can be enough to make photos stand out against a neutral background.

(Left) A beautiful window frame pulls the view outside into the room, making it an integral aspect of the interior design. A frame can do the same for your photographs.

Customize with paint.

Paint is the fastest, cheapest way to turn a generic interior into a personal paradise. It's also an ideal way to transform mass-produced scrapbook materials into unique works of art. If you're just getting started, I recommend craft acrylics, which are inexpensive, and watercolors, which are versatile and forgiving.

Find unusual details.

A jeweled box, a sleek statuette, a brocade drape—interior designers know that the perfect detail can take a design from good to great. To make your scrapbooks unique, search for unusual elements or invent striking new ways to bring old favorites to your pages.

You may be surprised at the various layouts you can create when you accept the challenge of producing different designs while repeating a single element such as a certain color, shape, or motif.

Be inspired.

Look to art, architecture, the natural world, and the work of others to find new looks you can bring to your designs. If you're stuck for ideas, unlock your ingenuity by challenging yourself to use a single element in many different ways. Paradoxically, limiting your choices in one respect can help you discover new options.

Using the same stamp for many different layouts encouraged me to focus even more closely on how placement, color, line, and embellishment can make each page unique.

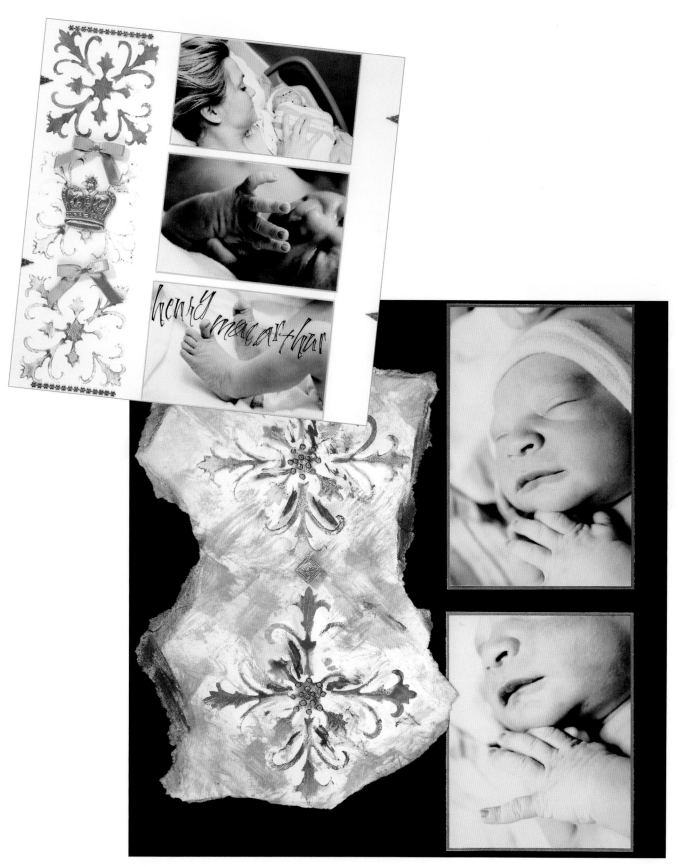

henry macarthur

PROJECT

Antique Scroll Motif

Materials

- Bronze and gold acrylic paints
- Scroll stamp
- Stiff brush
- Textured scrapbook paper

Instructions

STEP ONE

Use the scroll stamp to apply undiluted bronze and gold paint to the page.

STEP TWO

Blend one part each metallic bronze paint and gold paint to achieve a third color.

STEP THREE

Create a foreground by dabbing the three colors randomly, using a dry stiff brush.

STEP ONE

STEP TWO

STEP THREE

Scrapbookers often apply stamps as a final layer
to a page, but a range of new effects are possible
when you use them as a starting point.

Angel Art

Throughout this book, I've encouraged you to strike out and find the unique designs that are waiting to be discovered in your imagination. Yet from personal experience, I understand that designers help each other see different ways to make their work beautiful and interesting. For this reason, I created the following gallery of images for you to use in your personal pages. Feel free to enlarge them for use as background pages or shrink them to create embellishments or frames. Use them separately or combine them; use part or all of an image, as you wish. I invite you to make them your own.

Some people call work shared in this way "Angel Art." I like this expression—to me, it reflects the spirit of goodwill that can make creating such a satisfying experience. Your imagination is a gift, and I hope that by freely sharing my work with you, I inspire you to share your talent with as many people as you can.

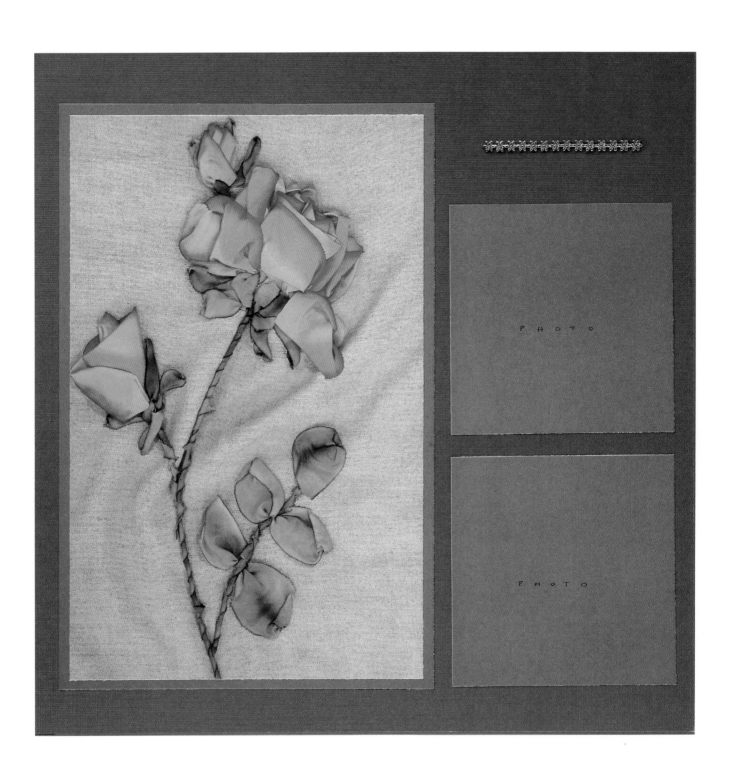

Pink Rose

Vintage Vogue

Green Wallpaper

Cheery Bedroom

BEBE

"ROAR"

Bebe Lion

Savannah

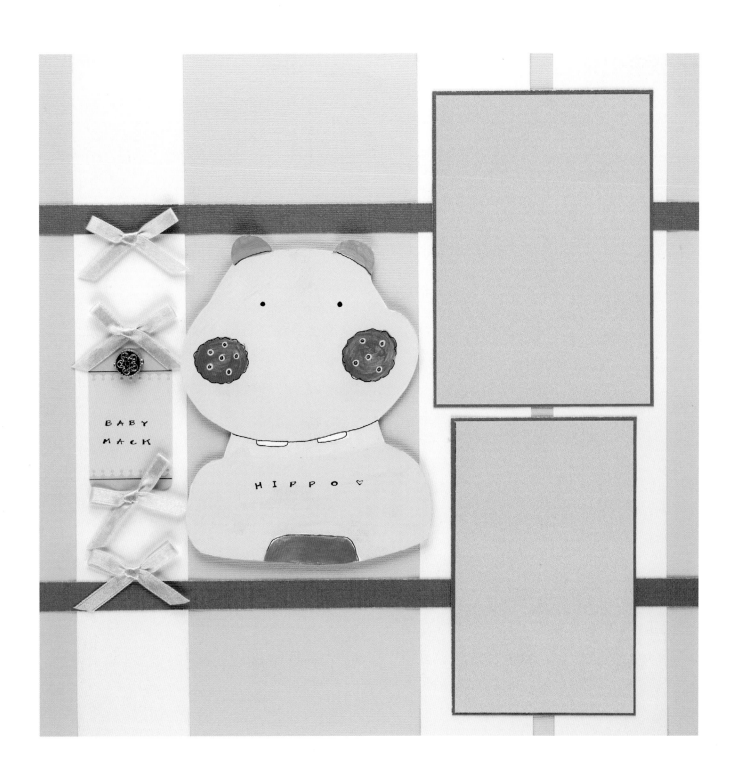

Baby Hippo

Seafoam

Grand Occasion

Lady's Parlor

HAPPY BIRTHDAY

Still Life

"Sweet Baby"

Sweet Baby

Flower Study

Country Drive

Antique Book

Delicate

Art Deco Dots

Italian Wall

Heart Circle 1

Heart Circle 2

Italian Villa

French Toile

Classical Frame

Tuscan Field

Matisse

122

Baby's Dress

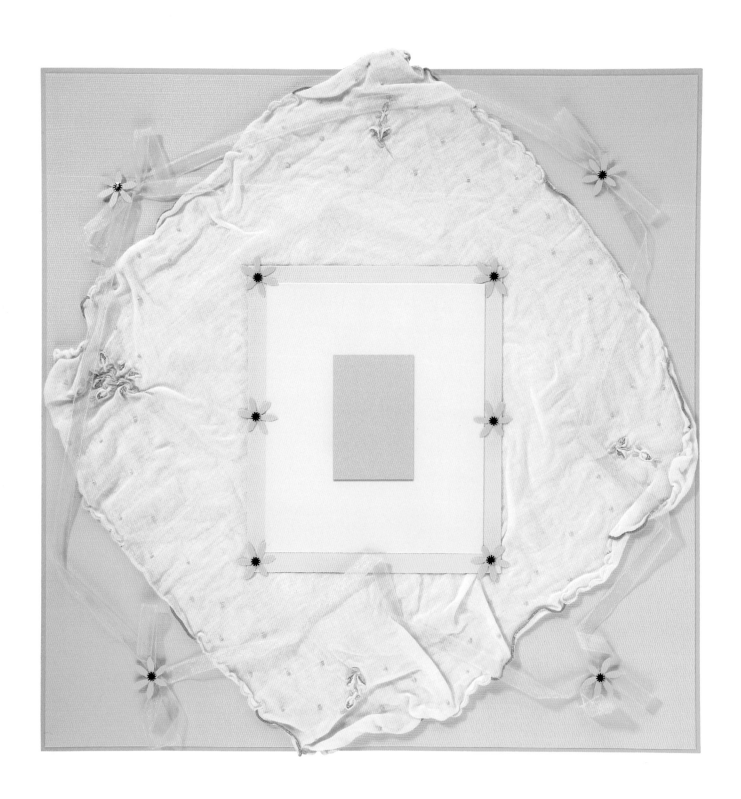

Pink Hanky

ACKNOWLEDGMENTS

In addition to being a designer and scrapbook artist, I am an athlete. I have run many races, and each time I cross the finish line, I realize yet again how many people helped me get there. In a sense, creating a book is like running a race; now, as I cross the finish line, I want to thank those who got me here.

I thank my Father in heaven, the ultimate Creator and Artist.

Mom, you have taught me everything I know. Your art captured my attention years ago, but your heart won me from the beginning.

Beloved David, you embody encouragement, and I would be nowhere without you. I love you with all my heart.

Baby Mack, you were my little trooper the whole way.

Special thanks to Sommer, Lana, G.G., and Jenn Gibbs. I could not have done any of this without you.

And thank you to the following photographers and studios who provided such fabulous images for me to work with: Carolyn Bauman Cruz, Cowboys and Angels, Donna Vance, Ira Montgomery Photography, Milburn's Portrait Art, Nancy Sherry, and Sommer Photography.

"Beloved."

CREDITS

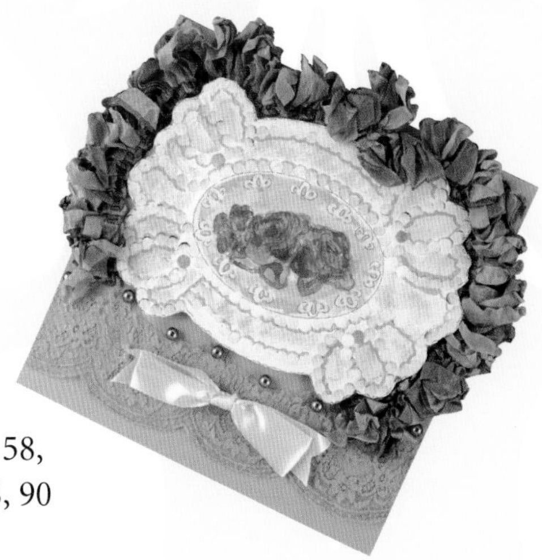

Editor: Jennifer Gibbs
Book Designer: Dan Emerson for Pinnacle Marketing
Graphic Designers: Ryne Hazen and Zachary Williams
Production Design: Richie Taylor
Illustrations: Kim Coxey
Heather Harcourt
Photographers: Cowboys and Angels, 3, 17, 24, 27, 31, 35, 54–55, 58, 60–61, 63, 66, 68, 72, 79, 88, 90
Donna Vance, 79
Milburn's Portrait Art, 48
Kevin Dilley, 4, 16
Mark Tanner, 32
Milburn's Portrait Art, 11, 38, 86
Nancy Sherry, 80
Scot Zimmerman, 28–29
Sommer Photography, 9–10, 12, 15–16, 18–19, 21–23, 25, 28, 32–34 36–37, 39, 41–42, 44–45, 48, 51, 57, 59, 64, 69, 71, 74–76, 80, 84, 87, 89, 91–93, 95–96, 126
Wanelle Fitch, 20, 24, 31, 43, 44, 76

METRIC CONVERSION CHART

inches to millimeters and centimeters						
inches	mm	cm	inches	cm	inches	cm
⅛	3	0.3	9	22.9	30	76.2
¼	6	0.6	10	25.4	31	78.7
½	13	1.3	12	30.5	33	83.8
⅝	16	1.6	13	33.0	34	86.4
¾	19	1.9	14	35.6	35	88.9
⅞	22	2.2	15	38.1	36	91.4
1	25	2.5	16	40.6	37	94.0
1¼	32	3.2	17	43.2	38	96.5
1½	38	3.8	18	45.7	39	99.1
1¾	44	4.4	19	48.3	40	101.6
2	51	5.1	20	50.8	41	104.1
2½	64	6.4	21	53.3	42	106.7
3	76	7.6	22	55.9	43	109.2
3½	89	8.9	23	58.4	44	111.8
4	102	10.2	24	61.0	45	114.3
4½	114	11.4	25	63.5	46	116.8
5	127	12.7	26	66.0	47	119.4
6	152	15.2	27	68.6	48	121.9
7	178	17.8	28	71.1	49	124.5
8	203	20.3	29	73.7	50	127.0

yards to meters									
yards	meters	yards	meters	yards	meters	yards	meters	yards	meters
⅛	0.11	2⅛	1.94	4⅛	3.77	6⅛	5.60	8⅛	7.43
⅛	0.11	2⅛	1.94	4⅛	3.77	6⅛	5.60	8⅛	7.43
¼	0.23	2¼	2.06	4¼	3.89	6¼	5.72	8¼	7.54
⅜	0.34	2⅜	2.17	4⅜	4.00	6⅜	5.83	8⅜	7.66
⅝	0.46	2½	2.29	4½	4.11	6½	5.94	8½	7.77
⅝	0.57	2⅝	2.40	4⅝	4.23	6⅝	6.06	8⅝	7.89
¾	0.69	2¾	2.51	4¾	4.34	6¾	6.17	8¾	8.00
⅞	0.80	2⅞	2.63	4⅞	4.46	6⅞	6.29	8⅞	8.12
1	0.91	3	2.74	5	4.57	7	6.40	9	8.23
1¼	1.03	3¼	2.86	5⅛	4.69	7¼	6.52	9⅛	8.34
1¼	1.14	3¼	2.97	5¼	4.80	7¼	6.63	9¼	8.46
1⅜	1.26	3⅜	3.09	5⅜	4.91	7⅜	6.74	9⅜	8.57
1½	1.37	3½	3.20	5½	5.03	7½	6.86	9½	8.69
1⅝	1.49	3⅝	3.31	5⅝	5.14	7⅝	6.97	9⅝	8.80
1¾	1.60	3¾	3.43	5¾	5.26	7¾	7.09	9¾	8.92
1⅞	1.71	3⅞	3.54	5⅞	5.37	7⅞	7.20	9⅞	9.03
2	1.83	4	3.66	6	5.49	8	7.32	10	9.14

INDEX